Some Birds Have Funny Names

by Diana Harding Cross

illustrated by Jan Brett

CROWN PUBLISHERS, INC.

NEW YORK

For Jean Mary

The text of this book is set in 18 point Baskerville
The illustrations are line drawings, with half-tone overlays,
prepared by the artist, for black and green.

Library of Congress in Publication Data
Cross, Diana Harding.
  Some birds have funny names.
  SUMMARY: Briefly describes certain habits or
characteristics which account for the popular
names of 14 North American birds.
  1. Birds—Juvenile literature.   2. Birds—
Nomenclature, Popular—Juvenile literature.
[1. Birds]   I. Brett, Jan, 1949-   II. Title.
QL676.2.C76   1981   598.297'012   80-28168
ISBN: 0-517-54005-3

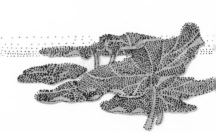

Contents

A bird's name
often tells
something about it.
The red-winged blackbird
is black and has
a red spot on each wing.
This bird's name
tells what it looks like.

Birds are also named
for what they eat,
for things they do,
or for the sounds they make.
The fourteen birds
in this book
can be found
in or near
North America.

Bufflehead

The bufflehead is a small
black-and-white duck
found on
lakes and rivers.
It has a big head
and almost no neck.
The shape of its head
made people think
of the buffalo.
So they named it
bufflehead.

10

When the bufflehead
is trying
to attract a mate,
it puffs out
its feathers.
This makes its head
seem even bigger!

CATBIRD

The catbird
imitates the songs
of other birds.

If different birds
are nesting near it,
the catbird will sing
one bird's song
a few times.
Then it will sing
another bird's song.
Catbirds can imitate
many sounds:
a person whistling,
a door creaking,
a frog croaking.
But the sound
a catbird makes most often
sounds like a cat's
mewing.
That is how
it got its name.

Cowbird

The cowbird is often found
among cows.
It stands on their backs
and eats the insects
that jump out
of the grass
as the cows graze.
Long ago
the cowbird followed
the buffalo herds
across the plains.
It was called
the buffalo bird then.

Some people think
the cowbird moved too often
to build a nest
so it laid its eggs
in other birds' nests.
Today there are not many
buffalo herds left
so cowbirds stay near cows.
But they still lay
their eggs
in strange nests.
Other birds
hatch the cowbird's eggs
and raise its chicks.

CROSSBILL

The crossbill lives
in the pine forests
of the North.

The upper and lower parts
of the crossbill's beak
cross at the ends.
This shape
is very useful.
The crossbill uses its beak
to twist open pinecones.
It then eats the seeds inside.
The crossbill often sits
on the pinecone
while it eats.
If you hear a snapping
sound in a tree,
it could be a
crossbill eating.

FLYCATCHER

The flycatcher often sits
on a branch
waiting for a fly.
When a fly comes by,
the flycatcher darts out
and snaps it up.
It often comes back
to the branch to eat.

The sharp feathers
around its beak
help trap insects.
Flycatchers are very fast.
They almost never miss a fly.

FRIGATEBIRD

Long ago
pirates sailed the seas
in fast ships
called frigates.
When sailors saw
a fast, strong seabird,
it made them think
of the pirates
and their ships,
so they named it
the frigatebird.
This bird sometimes acts
like a pirate.

It will swoop and dive
at a bird carrying food.
When the bird drops its food,
the frigatebird catches it
in midair
and gulps it down!
This bold bird
has also been called
the eagle of the sea
and the man-o'-war bird.

HUMMINGBIRD

The hummingbird's wings
move so fast that
they make a humming sound.
By beating its wings
very hard,
the hummingbird controls
its flying.
It can fly up and down
like a helicopter.
It can fly backwards.
It can even hang
in the air in one place.

Flying like this
helps the hummingbird
to eat its food.
It hangs in midair
and sticks its long pointed bill
into one flower
and then another.
It sucks up the nectar
inside.
All the while
you can hear the hum
of its beating wings.

OVENBIRD

The ovenbird makes its nest
on the forest floor
from fallen leaves
and broken twigs.
The nest has
a hidden door
and a smooth,
rounded roof.
The nest looked like an oven
to the New England settlers,
so they named the bird
that made it the ovenbird.
The ovenbird's nest
looks like
a pile of leaves.

When the ovenbird
lays its eggs
inside its nest,
they are safe
from other birds
and animals.

Oystercatcher

The oystercatcher lives
on the Atlantic coast.
It pokes its long red beak
into the wet sand.
When it finds a clam
or an oyster,
it opens the shell
with its sharp beak.
Then it eats the meat inside.
The oystercatcher finds
most of its food
near the shore
at low tide.

ROADRUNNER

The roadrunner runs along
the dusty roads
of Arizona and New Mexico.
Its long legs, big feet,
and long tail
keep it balanced
when it runs.
The roadrunner can run
faster than most people
and faster than its enemies.
Though it can fly,
it usually doesn't.

It finds its food on the ground.
It chases snakes,
mice, lizards, and
other small animals.
When it catches them
in its big beak,
it swallows them whole!

SNAKEBIRD

The snakebird lives
in the swamps
of the South.
Like many other water birds,
the snakebird eats fish.
When it swims,
its long black neck
wiggles like a snake.
That's why it's called
the snakebird.

This bird is a good swimmer
and diver.
When its feathers
get very wet,
it flies to a nearby tree.
Then it spreads
its big wings
and dries them
in the sun.

SPOONBILL

The spoonbill's long bill
is flat at the end,
just like a spoon.
When it goes wading
in the salt marshes
of Texas and Florida,
it moves its bill
from side to side
and lifts tiny
fish and shrimp
out of the water
and eats them.

The spoonbill's long legs
are good for wading.
This bird's full name
is roseate spoonbill
because its body
is a bright rosy pink.

TUBENOSE

A tubenose bird has tubes
on each side of its bill.
It uses them
in two strange ways.
When it swallows a fish
and takes in water,
it shoots the water out
through its tubes.
When the tubenose
is looking for food
and other birds
come too close,

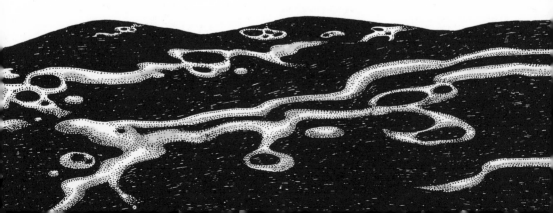

it shoots a hot
waxy oil at them.
The other birds
fly away.
Then the tubenose
has all the room it needs
to look for food
in the sea.

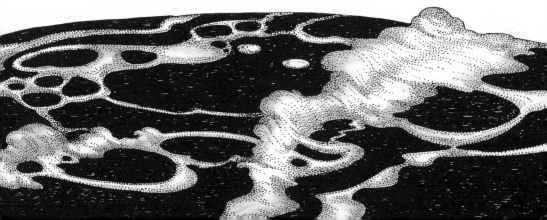

Woodpecker

The woodpecker pecks at trees
with its hard sharp bill
to find ants and beetles
under the bark.
Then it laps them up
with its long sticky tongue.
Sometimes the woodpecker
drums on trees
to let other birds
know where it is.
Sometimes it drums
for no special reason.

In the spring
the woodpecker pecks
a large deep hole
in a tree.
It is making a nest.
It lays its eggs
inside the hole
on a soft bed of wood chips.

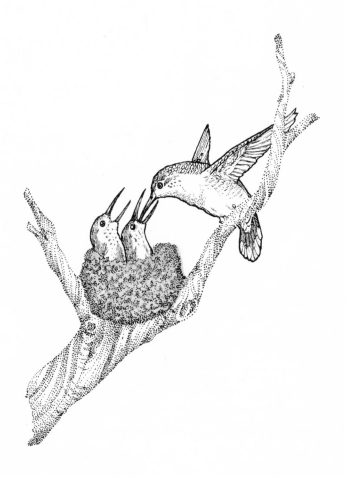